Tales o_ Dorset Coast

By Robert Hesketh

ISBN: 978-0-9928073-3-7

Inspiring Places Publishing
2 Down Lodge Close
Alderholt
Fordingbridge
Hants
SP6 3JA

Contents

Introduction

Dorset's rich maritime history is well seasoned with salty characters, whose fascinating stories show various ways the sea has given Dorset its living through war and peace – both within and outside the law. Indeed, the colourful careers of Dorset seamen such as Harry Paye, Henry Strangways and Isaac Gulliver prove how nice distinctions between smuggling and trade; piracy and privateering; personal profit and national interest were often blurred.

Trade and England's defence encouraged the development of Dorset's ports, havens on an exposed and sometimes treacherous eighty-eight mile long coast which has one of Europe's greatest densities of shipwrecks. Poole, Weymouth, Portland, West Bay and Lyme led the way and each has its story to tell. Smaller ports and harbours such as Swanage and Winspit were used chiefly by quarrymen and fishermen, whilst smugglers landed their contraband on secluded beaches and coves all along the Dorset coast too.

Smuggling grew to be Dorset's leading industry in the eighteenth and nineteenth centuries. It gained a patina of adventure and romance, though the harsh social conditions from which it grew and the violence and intimidation that often characterised it should not be forgotten.

Below: Lulworth Cove is one of the most well known locations on the Dorset coast. Still part of a large estate, it has remained largely unchanged for hundreds of years and was once a favourite haunt of smugglers.

Just as smuggling declined in the mid-nineteenth century, seaside holidays came to the rescue of Dorset's coastal economy. Weymouth was Dorset's first resort, thanks to George III's patronage and a growing faith in the health benefits of sea bathing. Later, railways and paddle steamers made travel to the Dorset coast cheap and fast as never before and tourism grew to be the Dorset coast's leading industry.

Picture: Freshwater Bay on the Isle of Portland from disused quarries. The Romans quarried the Portland Stone here and it was used in the construction of Exeter Cathedral in the fourteenth century. The stone became well known internationally after Sir Christopher Wren used it in rebuilding St Paul's Cathedral following the Great Fire of 1666.

The Historic Background

The Iron Age

Iron Age Dorset was part of an international maritime network. Poole harbour is the oldest port in north-west Europe, with substantial stone and wood remains at Clavel Point dating from 250BC. The Durotiges who inhabited Dorset and gave the county its name engaged in trading with the Veneti of Brittany, whilst local trade is evidenced by the 10m (33ft) long Poole logboat. Made from a single oak tree and dating from 295BC, it is housed in Poole Museum.

Trade demanded defence. Hengistbury Head was a major port, as its massive defensive ditches, the "Double Dykes", testify. Similarly, fortifications at Flower's Barrow and Bindon Hill guarded Worbarrow Bay and Lulworth Cove respectively.

The Roman and Saxon Periods

Arriving in 43AD, the Roman invaders recognized a superb natural harbour when they saw one and established Hamworthy just west of Poole, using it throughout their occupation of Britain. Poole was included in the Anglo-Saxon kingdom of Wessex and used as a fishing base and anchorage for ships on their way to the new stronghold of Wareham. Viking raiders first attacked England in 787 and remained a major threat for over two centuries. In 836 "fought King Egbert with thirty-five pirate ships at Charmouth, where great slaughter was made, and the Danes remained masters of the field". The next

Hengistbury Head and Christchurch Harbour.

Above: Swanage with remains of the old pier in the foreground. Swanage developed as a port in Victorian times, exporting the local Portland Stone.

year *The Anglo-Saxon Chronicle* gloomily noted: "Ealdorman Aethelhelm fought against the Danes at Portland with the men of Dorset and the ealdorman was slain, and the Danes had possession of the place of slaughter."

King Alfred harboured ships at Lyme in 840, but the Danes struck again in 876, capturing Wareham. Alfred made peace with them, yet the Vikings broke their oath, evaded the English levies and struck Exeter, although they lost 120 ships en route in a storm off Swanage. Vikings attacked Portland again in 982 and sailed up the Frome in 998. In 1015 King Cnut (also known as Canute) led a second Viking raid along the Frome and "harried in Dorset, Wiltshire and Somerset".

The Medieval Period

Whilst the Viking menace receded, the Dorset coast remained vulnerable to attack. Realizing this, England's new Norman masters built castles at Christchurch, Wareham and Church Ope Cove on Portland.

French attacks were frequent, especially during the Hundred Years War (1377-1453). As part of a series of raids, Lyme and Poole were attacked in 1377 and Melcombe Regis burnt and destroyed. Portland was attacked in 1404; the English retaliated by burning forty Norman settlements.

Pirates and Privateers

Harry Paye: Villain or Hero?

Retribution descended on Poole in 1405. Two French and three Spanish galleys attacked and burnt the town, home port of Harry Paye - remorseless and profane pirate or courageous defender of England and benefactor of Poole, depending on one's point of view and nationality.

Both Spain and France had reason to seek revenge. Harry Paye, otherwise "Arripaye", took prisoners at will, ransoming them for money; led raids from Normandy to the Bay of Biscay and seized cargoes of iron from Bilbao. More infamously, he plundered and burnt Gijon in Spain in 1398, home of his lover, the Countess Isabel, carrying away the gold crucifix of Santa Maria de Finisterra.

To his French and Spanish foes Paye was a pirate, but the attitude of the English Crown appeared ambivalent. In 1402, he was one of several sailors from south coast ports charged with piracy. Only two years later, he was ordered to fit out privateers and attack the French coast.

In the ensuing attack Harry Paye's ship was captured by French sailors. He and his crew were held on deck by a few guards, while the rest of the French party went below looking for loot. Breaking free, Paye's men killed their captors as they emerged on deck. Seizing two French vessels, they sailed up the River Seine under the French flag, plundering several ships before escaping to sea.

When the Franco-Spanish force attacked Poole the next year, Harry Paye was at sea. According to a French report, the men of Poole "collected in some force, archers and men at arms". They "fought right well" and won their enemies' respect. However, they "were at length compelled to retreat,

Poole Quay.

leaving among the slain a brother of Arripaye's, a gallant man of arms, who distinguished himself by his great exertions before he fell".

Harry Paye's revenge came in 1407. Leading fifteen ships along the Channel, he captured twenty French merchant ships, which he brought back to Poole in triumph. It is said one seizure carried 12,000 gallons of fine wine – enough to keep Poole drunk for a month.

Privateers

From an English standpoint, Harry acted as a privateer. Privateers or "corsairs" were effectively a free enterprise navy. All the world's maritime powers, not least England and her arch enemy France, used privateers, especially as commerce raiders. Before states could afford regular navies, privateers were at the heart of national maritime defence. Privateering continued for centuries afterwards and only officially ended with the 1856 Declaration of Paris.

Self-financed and sailing their own ships, privateers were usually distinguished from pirates by carrying letters of marque from their respective governments – documents which might save their lives if they were taken prisoner. In some cases, privateers acted unofficially through the tacit support of rulers who wished to deny they were waging war. In the next century, England's Queen Elizabeth became the past mistress of this subterfuge.

Pirate or privateer, Paye unquestionably enjoyed the Crown's support for most if not all of his career, which he concluded as a commander in the Cinque Ports fleet, a prestigious post guarding the five south-east ports closest to the French coast. He died Sir Harry Paye at Faversham, Kent, in 1419 and is commemorated with a fine tomb there at the Church of St Mary of Charity.

Poole Quay, today popular with tourists.

Henry Strangways

Like Harry Paye, Henry Strangways blurred the distinction between piracy and privateering. Born of a well known Dorset county family, this "Gentleman Pirate" began his career in 1552, plying the Irish Sea in cahoots with the piratical Cornish Killigrews, using Portland Castle to store their loot.

Strangways was a successful pirate and two warships were prepared at Portsmouth to capture him. He is recorded as a prisoner in the Tower of London in 1555, but it seems influential friends secured his release. In 1559, Strangways was re-arrested with eighty of his men and sentenced to death, but mysteriously avoided execution.

That same year, 1559, he attacked and plundered Spanish ships. King Philip II of Spain was outraged and Strangways spent another perfunctory spell in jail, but was released again under the promise of good conduct. It was a promise he did not keep. Pardoned once again – this time by Queen Elizabeth herself – he died a free man in 1562. This Royal Pardon combined with the extraordinary and repeated leniency shown him by the authorities and his use of Portland Castle (a fort built for national defence under orders of Henry VIII) as a pirate den, all indicate that Henry Strangways was enjoying his piratical career with the full connivance of the state. Surely he was a privateer in all but name?

Below: Portland Castle, one of Henry VIII's series of forts built to counteract the threat from France in the sixteenth century. (courtesy English Heritage)

Studland Bay with Handfast Point and Old Harry Rocks in the background. The bay became a favourite anchorage for pirates in the fifteenth and sixteenth centuries, providing shelter, plenty of inns and corrupt local officials. Like the smugglers after them they found the hinterland of wild heaths ideal for the distribution of their goods. (photo Verity Hesketh)

Pirates Clinton Atkinson and Philip Boyte

Piracy, as distinct from privateering, directed against the merchant ships of England's national enemies, was widely practised in Dorset. Studland was first mentioned as a pirate haven in 1429, when the *James of Studland* and the *Welfare of Swanage* drove a foreign ship ashore and plundered her.

Piracy reached its height in Dorset early in Elizabeth's reign, when ports including Weymouth were known to shelter pirates and there were plenty of Dorset merchants ready to buy stolen ships and their cargoes from pirates. Shelter also came from the law: in one case a juryman at the trial of a suspected pirate admitted he dealt with pirates.

Meanwhile, the Queen was backing the plundering of Spanish ships by many of her leading sailors, including Francis Drake, whom she knighted shortly after his return from circumnavigating the world aboard *The Golden Hind*. Elizabeth's half share of the Spanish loot Drake brought home surpassed the rest of the Crown's income for the year 1580.

That same year, 1580, the Baltic ships *Sea Horse* and *Master of the Sea* were forcibly brought to Studland and their cargoes sold. Many other ships fell victim to the Studland pirates, who usually bribed the Vice Admiral of Dorset at Corfe Castle, before holding a "fair" to sell their stolen goods.

Clinton Atkinson and Philip Boyte of Portland may have congratulated themselves in 1580, capturing an Italian ship worth £1300 and selling her at Topsham and Weymouth. However, Boyte was caught and hanged, though Atkinson bribed his jailer and escaped.

Atkinson's luck ran out in 1583. He was one of several Dorset pirates hunted down and hanged after a crackdown on piracy led by William Aboroughe, Clerk to the Navy and Benjamin Gunson, gentleman, commanding the *Bark Talbot* and the *Unica*. Peace returned to Studland.

Development of Dorset's Ports

Poole emerged as Dorset's largest medieval port. The town gained its charter in 1248, giving it a mayor and exemption from some tolls and customs. In 1433 it was granted Port of the Staple status to pursue the highly lucrative wool trade. To protect it from a repetition of the 1405 attack, Poole was fortified with a wall, ditch and gatehouse.

Poole's greatest trading days began when the Newfoundland fisheries developed from the late fifteenth century and continued into the nineteenth century. Ships from Poole and Weymouth sailed to Newfoundland with salt and provisions, returning with salted cod for Spanish, Portuguese and Italian ports. They completed the triangle carrying Mediterranean olive oil, salt and fruit back to Dorset.

Although the River Brit was navigable at high tide by small vessels and a harbour was begun at West Bay around 1385, trade at Bridport was on a minor scale until the nineteenth century. However, it was a major supplier of ship's ropes. In 1213 King John ordered there be "made at Bridport by night and day as many ropes for ships both large and small as they could".

Below, previous page: Studland Heath, the immediate hinterland of Studland Bay, ideal for smugglers and pirates to transport their goods.
Below: Today West Bay is a popular tourist location as well as a working harbour. The harbour is entirely man made, scooped out of the mouth of the River Brit.

The Cobb at Lyme

Lyme gained a Royal Charter in 1284 and added "Regis" to its name. It developed into a major port thanks to the Cobb protecting its otherwise exposed beach. It is not known exactly how old this man made harbour is, but it was storm damaged in 1313 and 1377. It was rebuilt by driving rows of oak piling into the sea floor and placing rocks between.

Whilst Poole and Weymouth later focussed their international trade on North America, Lyme specialized in the African trade, exporting cloth and manufactures and importing ivory and redwood dyes. By James I's reign, Lyme was paying £5000 annually in port taxes.

Above: Lyme Regis. No natural harbour exists between Exeter and Weymouth; the construction of the Cobb enabled Lyme to become an important port.

During the eighteenth century, the Cobb was rebuilt in mortared masonry. As Lyme was the only protected harbour along a dangerous stretch of coast, the government recognized its strategic importance at a time of threatened French invasion and footed the repair bill when the Cobb was badly damaged in 1792. In 1818 Lieutenant Colonel Fanshawe made further repairs, returning after the Great Storm of 1824 to repair 232ft of pier and 447ft of parapet.

Fanshawe's work has stood the test of time. Although international trade migrated from Lyme and other Dorset harbours to deep water ports as ships grew bigger in the eighteenth and nineteenth centuries, the Cobb remained vital in protecting Lyme's coastal, fishing and leisure trades.

Weymouth and the Black Death

Meanwhile, Weymouth became a borough in 1252, as did its neighbour and rival Melcombe Regis (the centre of today's Weymouth) in 1280. Both prospered with the Channel and Baltic trades until the Black Death entered England through Melcombe Regis in 1348. Carried by a sailor from Gascony, this terrible plague – estimated to have killed a third of England's people – rapidly spread as townsmen fled the port.

Weymouth suffered another heavy blow in 1386, when French raiders pillaged the town. Weymouth and Melcombe lost out in the woollen trade to Poole, but in 1428 they gained valuable licences as pilgrim ports for Santiago da Compostela. The lucrative pilgrim trade exacerbated rivalry between Weymouth and Melcombe Regis, until the two were united under one government in 1571 and a bridge connected them in 1597.

Weymouth grew rich on the North America trade, sending up to forty ships per year, principally to Newfoundland. Many Newfoundlanders and New Englanders trace their roots to Dorset, some even to the *Charity* which took a hundred emigrants from Weymouth, Dorset to Weymouth, Massachusetts in 1645. Among other New World settlements with Dorset names are Weymouth, Nova Scotia; Poole, Kentucky and Lyme, Connecticut.

In 1794 Weymouth became a base for the Channel Island packet boats. The Channel Island trade, along with fishing and pleasure craft, are the mainstays of Weymouth's prosperity today.

Below: The old harbour, Weymouth.

War and Defence in the 16th and 17th Centuries

Fearing French invasion, Henry VIII ordered a series of forts built along England's south coast around 1540, including the twin forts of Portland Castle and Sandsfoot Castle opposite on the Weymouth shore. Portland Castle was strengthened to repel the Spanish Armada of 1588. In the event, English ships fended off the Spanish at the Battle of Portland.

With the Armada threatening, Queen Elizabeth's government charged Weymouth to provide two ships and a pinnace (ship's boat); Poole with one ship and a pinnace; Lyme, Chard and Axminster together with two ships and a pinnace. Alarmed at the cost, the Dorset ports haggled, but with the Armada near, Weymouth supplied six ships and Lyme two, whilst Poole supplied essential powder and shot.

Dorset was bitterly divided in the Civil War. Poole, Lyme and Weymouth supported Parliament, whilst the Royal Manor of Portland naturally fought for King Charles. The Bankes family, who held huge estates and the then intact Corfe Castle, were among Charles's most powerful Dorset supporters.

Portland Castle was taken and retaken several times before the Royalist defeat of 1646, but Lyme withstood an eight week siege by Prince Maurice in 1644, largely thanks to supplies sent in by sea from Parliament, which well understood Lyme's strategic importance. Protected by its medieval defences, Poole remained staunch for Parliament too. In 1646, Parliamentary forces from Poole marched on Corfe Castle. Having taken it despite a brave defence led by Lady Mary Bankes, Parliament ordered Corfe Castle's partial demolition. Poole was duly punished after the Restoration of Charles II, by having its defences destroyed.

Sandsfoot Castle. (English Heritage)

Above: Lyme Regis Harbour behind the famous Cobb.

The Menace of French Privateers

Local seamen distinguished themselves in two late seventeenth century actions against French privateers, a long standing menace along the Dorset coast. According to a contemporary account, Captain Peter Joliffe of Poole was cruising off Portland in 1794 when he saw a French privateer take a Weymouth fishing boat as prize. Although his small sloop rigged coaster was much smaller than the French vessel, he retook her prize and forced her onto shore at Lulworth, where local people made themselves masters of the ship and took her crew prisoner.

William Thompson, master of a Poole fishing boat, was attacked by a Cherbourg privateer the following year. Wisely, Thompson had equipped his boat with two small guns and small arms besides. This was not unusual, for English merchant vessels of all sizes were prey for privateers and also Barbary corsairs, notorious for selling sailors as slaves.

Thompson and his crew - one man and a boy - fought back. It is said they wounded eight of the French crew, who turned their ship about and made off with Thompson in pursuit. After firing on the French sloop incessantly for two hours, Thompson forced her surrender and brought the heavily armed vessel with its crew of sixteen back in triumph to Poole.

Joliffe and Thompson were awarded gold chains and medals. Thompson was allowed to keep his captured vessel and both were celebrated in a jingoistic song, "The Courageous Captain".

The Classic Smuggling Period, 1688-1815

Dorset has a long and fascinating history of smuggling, beginning in medieval times with the illegal export of England's main source of wealth, wool, which carried a heavy duty. Later, the export of wool was banned entirely. So much was wool smuggling feared by the authorities that it carried the death penalty, though most offenders were transported.

However, it was the illegal import of dutiable goods that made smuggling one of Dorset's chief sources of wealth during the classic smuggling period, 1688 to 1850. Indeed, smuggling was a major industry throughout Britain at that time, involving a network of shippers, financiers and distributors, reaching from the humblest strata of society to the highest. Because smugglers kept no books figures are lacking, but possibly a fourth of Britain's import/export trade was illegal. For some commodities, tea in particular, the figure may have been as high as two thirds.

War and smuggling went hand in glove, for the government's main sources of revenue to wage war were Customs and Excise duties. Indeed, the classic smuggling period began in 1688 with William III's wars with Louis XIV's France. Between then and the end of the Napoleonic Wars in 1815, Britain was at war for 67 out of 127 years. Smuggling thrived as duties were repeatedly raised.

Successive British governments sought to finance war - principally with the smugglers' main business partners, the French - through extortionate taxes on luxury goods, whilst the smugglers' strove to supply those goods cheaply and illegally, through "Free Trade". In the protracted struggle between smugglers and the Law, the smugglers generally had the best of things, especially in the early stages of the conflict, when contraband was often landed with impunity on open beaches or even surreptitiously offloaded at ports such as Poole and Christchurch under the very noses of Customs officers who, like Joshua Jeans of Christchurch (page 27) frequently colluded with the very men they were supposed to catch.

More often than not, the smugglers outwitted or outmanoeuvred their opponents. The picture of the clever underdog fooling the dull witted authorities is part of the enduring appeal of smuggling and is well illustrated in Thomas Hardy's smuggling tale *The Distracted Preacher*, set at Owermoigne on the Dorset coast. It is not the whole truth, as smugglers also resorted to violence and intimidation, an inevitable result of challenging the armed authority of the state.

Geography fostered Dorset's seafaring traditions, its host of sailors, boat builders and fishermen, who provided the skilled men and vessels

Above: Mupe Bay near Lulworth Cove. This part of the Dorset coast has long associations with smuggling. Still marked on the Ordnance Survey maps is "Smugglers Cave", situated at the bottom right of the picture. The area still presents as unspoilt and secluded as it is part of the army ranges, only open at certain times. (pg 47)

for smuggling contraband across the Channel. Dorset's many sandy bays, sheltered coves and the long, lonely stretch of Chesil Bank were all well suited for landing illicit cargoes unobserved. Moreover, Dorset had long established links and easy communications with its main suppliers of contraband – the Channel Islands and Brittany.

Smuggling had strong attractions for Dorset's rural poor, many impoverished and dispossessed by wholesale enclosures of common land during the eighteenth and early nineteenth centuries. At a time when those convicted of grand larceny (theft of goods valued above one shilling) could be and were often hung, smuggling offered much higher returns with a relatively low risk of punishment – which usually consisted of fines, the destruction of smuggling vessels or enforced service in the Royal Navy. Smugglers rarely suffered the death penalty for anything less than murder or aggravated assault. Undoubtedly, the greatest dangers they and all seamen faced was the sea itself. Poverty and a thirst for adventure meant there were plenty of people willing to flout Customs and Excise duties widely regarded as unjust and unwarranted. As *The Distracted Preacher* makes clear, few Dorset people considered smuggling a crime; many benefited from it and supported it, which greatly reduced the risk of capture for smugglers. Support and help in landing, hiding and distributing cargoes was especially strong among Dorset's markedly independent and tightly knit coastal communities. All along the Dorset coast in places such as Christchurch, Poole, Swanage, Weymouth, Chideock and Lyme communities were actively involved in smuggling and few would dare betray a smuggler for fear of ostracization and reprisal.

Smuggling was popular. To some, especially its often wealthy and outwardly respectable backers who commonly bought shares in a smuggling run in the same way as they might in a legal company, it brought considerable profit. For the crews of smuggling vessels, the landing parties and distributors, it raised life beyond mere subsistence based on farming, quarrying and fishing. Moreover, smuggling brought extortionately taxed luxuries including brandy, tea, silks, snuff and tobacco within the reach of almost everyone.

On gentle sandy beaches such as Studland and what is today Bournemouth, but was almost deserted sandy heathland until the area was developed as a Victorian resort, smugglers could land contraband directly. They had a harder task at Dorset's more inaccessible coves. Sometimes, men had to haul the contraband up steep cliffs. An alternative from some beaches was to carry the goods up narrow cliff paths, as described in J. Meade Faulkner's

Above: Christchurch Harbour. Few places were more suitable for the smugglers' trade; flanked by sandy beaches and with the wild hinterlands of the New Forest and Cranborne Chase for the transport and concealment of contraband.

Above: Quarried caves in Portland Stone at Winspit, used to store contraband?

Dorset smuggling novel, *Moonfleet* (1898). Modelled on East Fleet by Fleet Lagoon it, like *The Distracted Preacher*, contains a wealth of telling historical details. Brandy was often borne in two or four gallon barrels called ankers, slung fore and aft over a man's shoulders with rope – customarily provided by thoughtful French and Channel Island merchants, who also supplied other smuggling equipment as well as contraband. At the cliff top, a team of sure footed donkeys or ponies would be waiting.

With their hooves muffled, the pack animals processed silently through the night as Kipling envisaged (below) to deliver their goods to customers or to hide them. Hiding places ranged from hollow trees to safe houses, including churches such as Langton Matravers. Farmers' barns; specially constructed pits; hidden wall cavities in inns, as well as Purbeck's and Portland's numerous quarries and caves, were also used.

Rudyard Kipling deftly depicted a landing party at work, the community's complicity and the smugglers' respectable customers in "Smuggler's Song":

> *"Them that asks no questions isn't told a lie,*
> *Watch the wall my darling, while the Gentlemen go by!*
> *Five and twenty ponies*
> *Trotting through the dark –*
> *Brandy for the Parson,*
> *'Baccy for the Clerk..."*

Above: Langton Matravers Church. The roof of the church collapsed during a church service in the 1790s under the weight of 200 brandy kegs stored there. One worshipper was killed and several injured.

Smuggling grew and prospered between 1688 and 1815, the period Geoffrey Morley (see bibliography) describes as "the Golden Age" for the Free Trade. In successively raising duties and placing them on more and more goods – an astonishing 1,425 items by 1815 – the government made contraband highly profitable.

Consequently, smuggling was practised on a huge scale. In 1783 a parliamentary committee reported 300 English vessels continuously involved in smuggling – effectively a second merchant navy. This did not include foreign smacks, post office vessels, East Indiamen, fishing boats and even vessels of His Majesty's Navy – all of which were known to participate in illicit trading.

Brandy was the market leader for Dorset smugglers, as it was for their Devon and Cornish colleagues. That same year, 1783, excise men estimated that four million gallons (eighteen million litres) of brandy were smuggled into Britain annually, a fuddling six bottles for every adult. Like gin, brandy could yield a profit of 400-500%, amply justifying the risks involved in a smuggling run. Profits on tobacco sometimes reached tenfold during the Napoleonic Wars.

Many reports show smugglers acted with impunity. A typical one from the Collector of Customs at Weymouth in 1717 tells of three officers investigating smugglers on Chesil Bank being driven off by thirty men. Another from 1719 describes five smuggling luggers unloading at Worbarrow Bay and the goods sold openly on the beach.

The government responded with more laws. From 1718, the Hovering Acts were aimed at vessels loitering along the coast with intent to offload smuggled goods. Boats carrying more than four oars and suspect cargoes could be seized and sawn into three pieces. Free pardons were offered to smugglers who turned informants, but there were few takers.

Smuggling Acts of 1736 and 1746 escalated penalties. The names of known smugglers were published in the London Gazette in 1746. Any gazetted smuggler who did not surrender within forty days was automatically subject to death. Similarly, the penalty for harbouring a smuggler was death and whole communities could be fined for offences.

Of course, the government had throughout the option of undermining smuggling by slashing duties. However, because of the exigencies of war, this was only done intermittently and piecemeal. For instance, when Prime Minister William Pitt halved the duty on wine in 1786, wine smuggling was hit hard. Similarly, when he cut duty on tea from 125% to a mere 12 ½ %, tea smuggling was all but eliminated. Pitt also introduced income tax as a radical new wartime measure in 1799, but the government was forced to repeal it in 1816 after the war with France was won through vociferous protests by powerful moneyed interests.

Below: Picturesque Worbarrow Bay where five smugglers' ships landed in 1719.

The Attack on Poole Customs House

Whilst countless smuggling runs were made without confrontation or bloodshed, violence was inevitable as smugglers challenged the armed authority of the state. One of the most notorious incidents began with the attack on Poole Customs House in 1747. Nine members of the Hawkhurst Gang from Kent were subsequently hanged, but it was the torture and murder the gang committed after attacking the Customs House that chiefly provoked the authorities' fury.

The affair began with a seven hour long chase of a smuggling cutter *Three Brothers* by Captain William Johnson of Poole Revenue cutter HMS *Swift*. When *Swift* loosed its guns on the smugglers they surrendered. Johnson's men brought *Three Brothers* back to Poole, lodging a valuable cargo of contraband tea, brandy, rum and coffee in the Customs House.

Enraged, Thomas Kingsmill, chief of the Hawkhurst Gang, led a heavily armed and well mounted party of sixty smugglers across country. Encountering no resistance, they broke open Poole Customs House at night and took what they regarded as their property. Heading home, the gang breakfasted at the George Inn, Fordingbridge. Among the crowd cheering them on was a cobbler called Chater, who was thrown a bag of tea by a crony in the gang.

Above: Poole Customs House, site of the attack by the infamous Hawkhurst Gang. You can now enjoy a drink and a meal there amongst its period features.

Hearing of this, the Southampton Collector sent one of his officers, William Galley, to Fordingbridge. Chater knew of the £200 reward for turning King's evidence and set off with Galley. En route to the magistrates, the two stopped at the White Hart in Rowland's Castle, Sussex.

Alerted by the landlady and her sons, who were deep in the smuggling business, a gang of smugglers tied Chater and Galley to a horse and had much cruel sport torturing them. Eventually, they buried the half dead Galley and hung Chater before finally stoning him to death.

No doubt, the smugglers thought this barbarous retribution would discourage any other would-be informers. In this they failed. One of their number was taken some months later and turned King's evidence. A Royal Proclamation was issued, listing the names of the murderers and demanding they surrender. Additionally, £500 was offered to informers. Seven gang members were arrested and executed. Four were hung in chains as a fearful warning.

Shortly afterwards, Kingsmill and four other gang members were tried at the Old Bailey, charged with breaking into the Poole Customs House. Kingsmill and his lieutenant, William Fairall, were found guilty, despite their protests that they had committed no crime as the contraband was theirs, and fairly bought in Guernsey. They too were hung in chains in their home villages. Thus ended the Hawkhurst Gang.

The Death of Robert Trotman, Smuggler, 1765

Robert Trotman's gravestone in Kinson churchyard, Bournemouth, claims he was "barbarously murdered on the shore near Poole" in 1765. Trotman died in a violent confrontation between his smuggling gang and Preventives. Although contemporary reports of the incident show it was the smugglers who initiated the violence and three Revenue men were injured before any

shots were fired, the inquest into Trotman's death ruled he had been murdered – that conclusion no doubt influenced by local sympathies and two smugglers being on the jury.

Right: The grave of Robert Trotman.

The Battle of Mudeford, 1784

In July 1784 Captain Ellis of HMS *Orestes* observed a busy scene on Mudeford Quay. Some 300 people, including the crews of two smuggling luggers were unloading a huge contraband cargo of 120,000 gallons of spirits and 30 tons of tea, with the aid of residents of Mudeford, Stanpit and Christchurch, 50 wagons and nearly 300 horses.

Seeing *Orestes* and the two Revenue cutters supporting her, the smugglers beached their luggers and stripped them of valuable spars and sails. Ellis ordered out six ship's boats under Sailing Master William Allen, who called to the smugglers to surrender. He was met by a hail of fire and mortally wounded.

Still, the King's men came on and secured the luggers whilst the smugglers beat a retreat to the Haven House Inn from where they held off their enemies for many hours, firing from windows and doorways. Ellis fired the ship's guns at the inn, damaging the chimney, but could not force a surrender. Eventually, the Revenue and Navy men retired with their wounded and the smugglers' vessels, but without prisoners or contraband.

Several men were tried for William Allen's murder, but only one was convicted for lack of evidence. George Coombes was hung and later gibbeted at Haven Point, Mudeford.

Below: Mudeford Quay with the Haven House Inn on the far left. The Mudeford Ferry now operates one hour cruises where you can hear all about the battle.

Corruption, Collusion and Inefficiency

Had the senior Christchurch Customs Officer, Joshua Jeans, and his Riding Officers done their duty events at Mudeford might have taken a very different course. An Inspector sent from London after the Battle of Mudeford discovered that these officers had seen the smugglers' wagons assembling in Christchurch and warned their superior. Jeans had told them to go home to bed.

The Inspector also found that Jeans had failed to support his officers and even discouraged them from doing their duty several times before July 1784. Moreover, he forbade them from recording details of smuggling vessels and ordered them to keep away from Mudeford.

Following the Inspector's damning report; Joshua Jeans was drummed out of the Customs Service. Bursey, one of his junior officers, was also dismissed for taking a bribe of a hundred kegs of brandy after the battle to turn a blind eye on the contraband.

Billy Coombs and Hannah Sillers (Hell hath no fury...)

Hannah Sillers, "the protecting angel of all smugglers", was landlady of the Haven House Inn during the Battle of Mudeford and a witness at the trial. Shortly afterwards, she moved to The Ship in Distress at nearby Stanpit, where her name is recalled in "Mother Sillers Channel". Hannah bought what she needed directly from the smugglers and provided them with refreshment. From Stanpit they set off on a dense network of inland routes.

A handsome widow famed for her raven black hair, Hannah fell in love with smuggler Billy Coombs, master of the *John and Susannah*, a swift 100 ton lugger armed with fourteen cannon and often used as a privateer. He promised to give up smuggling, marry her and become landlord of the Ship in Distress.

On Billy's last smuggling run, Hannah discovered he had made a similar promise to a young lady in Hamble. Hell hath no fury like a woman scorned; Hannah told the Preventives where and when to expect Billy's return. Sailing blithely into Christchurch Bay, Billy was ambushed by the Preventives aboard HMS *Osprey*. Battle between the two ships lasted three hours. Without Billy's orders, someone aboard the battered and dismasted smuggling lugger hauled down her colours to signal surrender, but his men continued firing. This breach of the accepted rules of engagement was Billy's death sentence at his trial; he was hanged at Lepe, just across Southampton Water from his home port of Hamble.

Violence on Bournemouth Beach

Bournemouth beach witnessed a violent confrontation between smugglers and Preventives in 1787. Captain Sarmon of the Cowes Revenue cutter *Resolution* spotted smugglers unloading contraband brandy and tea. He ordered his Mate, Thomas Quick, to lead an armed party in the jolly boat to recover the goods, which so frightened the smugglers that they ran off – only to return with reinforcements.

Quick roared at the smugglers to stand off or his men would fire. Replying they were determined to regain their property, the smugglers charged into a hail of fire. Those who survived fought the Preventives and made off with their cargo.

John Bishop, the smugglers' leader, was later brought to trial. Quick was too badly shocked and wounded to identify Bishop. However, his crewman Anderson, who had had his teeth smashed out with a pistol, was not and Bishop was duly hanged for smuggling, assault and carrying arms.

Above: Bournemouth beach, the scene of a violent confrontation.

More Corruption and Collusion

While some Revenue officers risked their lives, others considered discretion the better part of valour. Describing his schooldays in Christchurch in the 1770s, Richard Warner recalled "a flood of homely jokes poured upon them (the Revenue men) by the passing ruffians, but these were always accompanied by a present of kegs".

Joshua Jeans was evidently not the only officer who lent active assistance to smugglers. In 1788 a smuggling vessel was boarded at Poole and a detailed map was found showing the patrol areas of the customs vessels. It had been drawn by the Deputy Controller of Poole.

Warren Lisle, the unusually zealous former Collector of Customs at Weymouth, felt free to expose corruption in the Revenue service after retiring from a long and distinguished career. He reported to the Prime Minister in 1782 that the four Revenue cutters operating between St Alban's Head in Dorset and Berry Head near Brixham "...agree with the smugglers and content themselves with a small part from the smuggler, suffer the greater part to be run on shore".

Above: The Smugglers' Inn, Osmington Mills, headquarters of "French Pete".

The Charles Family and French Pete

Not all Preventives shirked their duties. Newly appointed Revenue Officer John Tallman was determined to catch the notorious French smuggler, Pierre La Tour, otherwise "French Pete", who was reputed to offload contraband at Osmington Mills from his fast cutter *L'Hirondelle*. Tallman naively pumped Emmanuel Carless, landlord of what is now the Smugglers' Inn, for information about La Tour. Carless span him hair raising tales of La Tour's bold deeds, before announcing the Frenchman had just dropped anchor and was heading to the bar. Alarmed, Tallman asked the landlord to hide him until he could call for reinforcements. Carless suggested the chimney was the very place.

La Tour and his men found an unusually cool reception from Carless, who put a finger to his lips and rolled his eyes towards the fireplace, remarking it was chilly for the season. Taking the hint, La Tour asked him to light the fire. Soon, a choking and humiliated Tallman was flushed out and sent on his way with laughter ringing in his ears.

Pierre La Tour married Arabella, Emmanuel's daughter and retired happy and rich to France. Meanwhile Emmanuel's son, Richard, was captured by Customs officers on a smuggling run aboard *Integrity* in 1828 and sentenced – as many sailor smugglers were – to naval service.

Emmanuel claimed his poor boy was of "consumptive habit of body and decaying constitution" and had been sailing for the benefit of his health. Affidavits from two surgeons backed this claim, but the authorities declared they were "quite assured that there never was an individual sent to the Navy under similar circumstances so fit and able as he". Moreover, they were convinced *Integrity* was not a fishing smack as claimed, but used exclusively for smuggling and that "no other vessel similarly employed has been so successful".

Having served his naval stint, Richard returned to his old ways. He was buried in Cherbourg in 1835, where his epitaph claims he was "inhumanely shot…by a Coastguard off the Isle of Purbeck".

In all, twenty-seven of the extended Carless family (also known as Charles) were fined for smuggling, served time either in Dorchester Gaol or (arguably more disagreeable) in the Royal Navy. Most later appear on the electoral rolls having gained a vote as landowners.

Smugglers and the Armed Forces

Pay and conditions were poor and discipline brutal in the armed forces and recruitment a chronic problem. Thus the authorities resorted to the press gang and enforced service for convicted smugglers – who often had the sailing skills the Navy needed.

Confronted with the American War of Independence, the British government was desperately short of fighting men. Thus, it offered a remarkable deal to smugglers with the 1782 Act of Oblivion. A smuggler who could find one landsman and one seaman for His Majesty's armed forces would escape a penalty up to a £500 fine. In exchange for two red jackets and two tars he could avoid any legal punishment, however great.

Isaac Gulliver

Isaac Gulliver, Dorset's most successful smuggler, was a major beneficiary of the 1782 Act. At this time he was said to have fifty men and fifteen smuggling luggers at his command, with operations reaching from the New Forest to the Cornish border and fortified headquarters at his house in Kinson, where he used the nearby church tower to store contraband and keep a watch on the Revenue. Legend has it that when the Revenue were hot on his trail, Gulliver was "buried" at Kinson churchyard with a mock funeral, only to continue his career in a variety of Dorset and Devon locations.

He was "one of the greatest and most notorious smugglers in the west of England", according to a Customs House report from Poole. However, the report continued: "In the year 1782 he took the benefit of His Majesty's proclamation for pardoning such offences and as we are informed dropped that branch of smuggling and afterwards confined himself chiefly to the wine trade".

Gulliver had no more intention of giving up his old trade than Henry Strangways had of abandoning privateering (page 9). His outwardly respectable business as a Teignmouth wine merchant was perfect cover for selling contraband. It is probable he used his smuggling connections with France to gather strategic information about the French Navy and coastal defences for the British government in return for immunity. Collusion with Gulliver included the business community too. William Fryer, a Wimborne banker, was his financier and later son-in-law.

In 1800, at the height of the Napoleonic Wars, Gulliver is said to have run one of his largest and most profitable contraband cargoes ashore near where Bournemouth Pier now stands. Evidently, he continued to prosper legally and illegally and died in 1822, leaving a very substantial estate of £60,000 and properties scattered across the West Country. He ended his days a respected citizen of Wimborne and was buried in the minster church.

Eggardon Hill: Isaac Gulliver owned a farm here and planted trees as a navigation aid for his ships. The hill is easily visible from the sea.

The Easton Massacre, 1803

Some were less fortunate in their dealings with authority than Isaac Gulliver. Five people were killed by the press gang at Easton on Portland in 1803 during a confrontation between thirty heavily armed men from the frigate HMS *Eagle* and local inhabitants.

The *Eagle's* captain landed his force early whilst the people of Easton were still asleep. They attempted to impress Nicholas Way who, as captain of a local vessel, was exempt from naval service. Woken by the furore, villagers ran hither and thither. One, Zachariah White, demanded to know what authority the press gang had. The sailors flourished a warrant from the Mayor of Weymouth – which was invalid on Portland. Tempers rose as the Navy men tried to snatch a second villager. *Eagle's* captain fired his pistol and his crew followed suit, killing three men instantly. Another man and a young woman, Mary Way, were fatally wounded. The sailors retired to the *Eagle* with one forced recruit. Charges were brought against them, but no convictions secured. Mary Way died nineteen days later with a bullet lodged in her back.

The Scientific Age of Smuggling, 1815 - 50

Napoleon was finally defeated in 1815. Once peace was secured the Royal Navy took over the Revenue cutters and led a renewed fight against smuggling. Marshalling its warships into a new Channel blockade against contraband rather than the French between 1816 and 1831, the Navy captured many smugglers and their boats – including a record 875 vessels in one year. Revenue hauls of contraband also increased impressively.

Largely manned by ex-servicemen, the Coastguard was formed in 1822. It was not the search and rescue organization of today, but a militarised anti-smuggling organization operating at sea and on land. They operated in force: sixteen Coastguards were stationed at Swanage in 1822, whilst the 1851 census shows ten out of thirty-seven households was headed by a Coastguard at Worbarrow Bay. In patrolling the Coast Path on foot and on horseback the Coastguards left a 630 mile long memorial to their work in the West Country stretching from Poole to Minehead.

With such vigorous opposition, smugglers were forced to adopt more secretive and cunning means of evasion during what Geoffrey Morley described as "The Scientific Age of Smuggling" – as opposed to the pre 1815 "Golden Age". These included weaving contraband tobacco into ship's rope and sewing it into sailors' clothing; building hidden compartments and hollowing out spars and masts in smuggling vessels to hide contraband. More contraband was hidden amongst legal cargoes and landed at regular ports.

The South West Coast Path: Today thousands of walkers enjoy this 630 mile footpath around the coast of Dorset, Devon, Cornwall and Somerset. It originated as a path for Coastguard patrols on the lookout for smugglers and much of its charm lies in the fact that it follows the coast so closely - a necessary requirement for the patrols to be able to look into every bay.

Another tactic was to use smaller, less conspicuous boats for smuggling, such as fishing smacks or coasters, rather than blatantly purpose built smuggling luggers. Using foreign vessels, which were largely immune from prosecution in English courts, was also successful.

When the "Philistines" (Preventives) were too close, rafts of brandy and gin kegs were weighted and hidden below water level close to shore – a process known as "sowing the crop". They were later recovered with grappling irons, often under the pretence of crab fishing, the goods being hidden beneath a perfectly legal catch.

Thus by various ingenious methods, vast quantities of smuggled goods continued to pour into England until the mid-nineteenth century, when the government itself adopted "Free Trade" as an article of economic faith and thereby destroyed the foundations of smuggling. "Free Trade", the very cause smugglers claimed to espouse (or the excuse they made for their crimes), ended the classic era of smuggling. Profits largely evaporated when duties were cut, especially on the mainstays of the business such as spirits, tea and tobacco.

William Lewis, Smuggler and Lieutenant Knight, Coastguard

Violent confrontations continued. William Lewis was killed by a shot from the schooner HMS *Pigmy*, 21st April 1822, aged 33 years according to his memorial in Wyke Regis churchyard. Above is a beautifully carved scene in which His Majesty's Revenue schooner *Pigmy* attacks *Active*, a smuggling cutter and blows away her sails with gunfire. When chased and then ordered to lower their sails, the crew of *Active* had complied, but a shot was nonetheless fired from *Pigmy* and that killed William Lewis. The inquest found he had been murdered and the shot had been "wantonly and maliciously fired".

By contrast, a Weymouth gravestone commemorates a murdered Coastguard:

Sacred to the memory of Lieut. Thomas Edward Knight R.N. of Folkestone, Kent, aged 42, who in execution of his duty as Chief Officer of the Coastguard was wantonly attacked by a body of smugglers near Lulworth on the night of 28th June 1832, by whom after being unmercifully beaten he was thrown over the cliff near Durdle Door from the effects of which he died the following day.

Thomas Hardy's The Distracted Preacher

Rich in historic details, Thomas Hardy's *The Distracted Preacher* gives a gentler picture of the cat and mouse game between a Dorset smuggling community and the Preventives in this later period. Richard Stockdale, a naïve and priggish Wesleyan preacher, takes up his new appointment in Nether

Moynton (Owermoigne). He is shortly enamoured of Lizzy, his charming young landlady – but finds himself in a moral quandary when he realizes she, like most of the village including his congregation, is an active smuggler. Moreover, Lizzy is one of the main financiers of the smuggling operations and she has no qualms about the work that brings excitement to her dull life and enables her to look after her infirm old mother.

Stockdale protectively follows Lizzy on her daring night time rendezvous with smuggling vessels and watches her signal them when the Preventives are near. Though his religious scruples prevent him from actively assisting Lizzy and the rest of the community in smuggling, he does not side with the Excise men when they search the village and seize contraband hidden in the church and a secret cavity under a tree.

All's well that ends well: the villagers recover their confiscated brandy kegs without harming the Philistines, who decide they've had enough of serving the King after being tied up by a party of tall strapping "women" with blackened faces. Lizzy eventually repents and marries Stockdale – though Hardy preferred his alternative ending in which Lizzy slipped away to America with Jim, the chief smuggler.

Below: Lulworth Cove, Hardy's 'Lulstead Cove' in "The Distracted Preacher".
The cove is a six and a half mile walk from Owermoigne where the story is set.

Shipwreck and Storm

The sea itself remained the greatest danger for all mariners, as the dramatic end of Slippery Rogers the Christchurch smuggler shows. Richard Warner recalled how he and his schoolfellows cheered bold Rogers when he sailed for France in his splendid purpose built smuggling vessel, 120 feet long with berths for the crew and space for two or three thousand ankers (small barrels) of spirits.

Rogers and his high spirited and usually well-oiled crew were "perfectly heedless of the weather", actually preferring rough seas when the Revenue cutters would stay in port. They set out from Le Havre on their last run, despite a rising storm. Attempting to meet the landing party at Hengistbury Head their fine galley was wrecked and many of them drowned.

Many wrecks show the savagery of the sea, but none more so than the 1882 wreck of *Alexandrovna*, a 1,250 ton Liverpool sailing ship driven onto Ragged Rocks west of Swanage by a hurricane. Such was the storm's force that it took only the ten minutes needed for rescuers to reach the spot for the ship to be reduced to matchwood and all the 77 crew drowned.

Halsewell, an East Indiaman wrecked in 1786, was the most notorious Dorset shipwreck and captured the nation's sympathy. Aboard were a full crew, returning soldiers and other passengers. Captain Pearce was accompanied by his two daughters and intended this to be his last voyage

Below: Winspit - the Halsewell was wrecked near here in 1786.

before retiring. It was. A storm drove *Halsewell* broadside on against a cave in the cliff face at Seacombe. Many scrambled to what they thought was safety, but the cliff above was almost impossible to climb and only two sailors made it to the top to alert rescuers from Worth Matravers. Many left behind succumbed to cold and exhaustion, or were washed away by the cruel sea. Although 82 people were eventually rescued 160 died, including Captain Pearce who refused to abandon his daughters.

Above: The Pilot Boat Inn in Lyme Regis, home to the Lassie legend?

Of all the storms that have struck the Dorset coast, the Great Storm of 1824 was the most terrible. Many ships were wrecked, including *Carvalho*, lost with all hands at Fleet, where the church was almost completely destroyed along with many houses. Fortunately, villagers saw the storm breach Chesil Bank and fled to safety on high ground at Chickerell. They returned to find the sloop *Ebenezer* standing on top of Chesil Bank like the Ark on Mount Ararat.

Many died in coastal communities, including "upwards of thirty" Portlanders, caught by a tidal wave. Among the bodies recovered was a man, his wife and seven children. As well as burying their friends and neighbours, locals buried the battered remains of countless sailors.

One tragedy was partly redeemed by a faithful dog. HMS *Formidable* was torpedoed in 1915 by German submarines during an exercise in the English Channel, her huge outline an easy target under the bright moon. Waterlogged and with no power, it was impossible to launch all *Formidable's* lifeboats. Many of the crew scrambled over her sides into the freezing water and 540 were lost. Survivors and dead crewmen were brought to the Pilot Boat Inn, Lyme Regis. One sailor taken for dead was brought back to consciousness when Lassie, the landlord's dog, licked his face. It is probably no coincidence she bore the same name as Eric Knight's 1940 novel *Lassie Come Home,* which was filmed in 1943.

Wrecking and Looting

Countless ships have been wrecked along the Dorset coast. "Wrecking", in the sense of looting cargoes from wrecked ships rather than deliberately luring them to their destruction, has been recorded down the centuries. Looting remained commonplace until the late nineteenth century – and continues in modern times, as the looted wreck of MSC *Napoli* just over the Devon border at Branscombe in 2007 proved.

Wrecks were long regarded as a godsend by impoverished coastal communities. In 1371, a hundred people were tried for robbing the Welfare, a Dartmouth ship carrying gold cloth and silks driven aground at Kimmeridge. Abbot Thomas of Cerne was among those convicted. Two centuries later, nothing had changed. *San Salvador*, an Armada galleon carrying the Spanish Paymaster-General and most of his gold, was wrecked before Old Harry Rocks in 1588. She drew local plunderers like flies to a honeypot.

Clergy in coastal parishes were required to read a 1713 Act "to better protect the fate of vessels in distress and their cargoes" to their flocks four times each year and remind them of the penalties they risked if prosecuted. It seems to have had little effect. As with smuggling, the authorities faced determined and sometimes violent local opposition. In 1716 Customs men failed to recover the cargo of *Jesus Maria Joseph* from Chesil Beach because looters "Beat, Hounded and Resisted us in the Salvidge."

Below: Old Harry Rocks near Studland, the site of many shipwrecks.

Above: Chesil Beach and the Fleet seen from Portland. The eighteen mile long shingle storm beach has seen many shipwrecks and its fierce undertow has dashed the hopes of many who thought they had reached land safely. At times injured survivors were left lying on the beach as locals looted the spilt cargoes.

When De Hoop ran aground on Chesil Beach in 1749 with £30,000 in gold and other valuables aboard, ten thousand wreckers are estimated to have come from all over Dorset and beyond, spending ten frenzied days turning over the pebbles for treasure. Armed soldiers were summoned to disperse the mob; much of the booty was recovered and several local men brought to trial. Augustin Elliot, a Portland labourer, was one. Charged with stealing 10ozs of gold and 20ozs of silver he was acquitted after a trial lasting six hours. As was pointed out later, empanelling a Dorset jury which did not contain looters then would have been nearly impossible.

Among the long, long catalogue of looted ships was *Royal Adelaide*, wrecked at Chesil Cove in 1872. The Coastguard got a rocket line to the distressed ship and all but seven of the crew and passengers were saved. While many of the crowd helped with the rescue, others were eager for plunder. Unfortunately, this included barrels of spirit. Five people died of alcoholic poisoning and hypothermia on the beach that November night.

War and Defence in the 19th and 20th Centuries

Dorset continued to play an important role in Britain's naval defence during the nineteenth and twentieth centuries. The county celebrated Nelson's victory at Trafalgar in 1805, in which 186 Dorset sailors served. At Burton Bradstock, one of many coastal communities where a volunteer regiment was formed to repel the threat of French invasion, the squire's family was so delighted their son was safe they opened a barrel of beer for the community. The church bells rang out and one drunken ringer broke the ropes.

Major work began on Portland Breakwater in 1847 in response to the perceived threat of French invasion, which remained part of British strategic planning until the 1890s. A huge team of engineers and craftsmen, backed by convict labour from the new Portland prison, were engaged on the project, which drew crowds of admiring visitors and the patronage of Prince Albert. Complemented by Nothe Fort and Verne Citadel, Portland Breakwater was considered complete in 1872.

Germany with its rapidly expanding navy came to be seen as a greater threat than France. In response, Portland's naval defences were upgraded between 1895 and 1906, making it the world's largest artificial harbour. The programme was completed in 1914 when the obsolete HMS *Hood* was sunk across the harbour entrance to seal it against attack.

Below: Nothe Fort at the entrance to Weymouth Harbour. It was commissioned in 1860 because of the perceived threat from France. It didn't see action against an enemy until World War Two. (Photo courtesy The Nothe Fort.)

The most notable attack came in July 1940, when 26 Stukas dive bombed and sank HMS *Foylebank* in Portland Harbour, killing 176 of the crew. Mortally wounded, Jack Mantle won the Victoria Cross by staying to fire at the Stukas until he fell.

Dorset's finest military hour came in 1944, playing a major role in the Normandy landings. Eighty-one landing craft sailed from Poole, making it the third largest D Day embarkation point, whilst nearly half a million troops and 144,000 vehicles embarked from USNAAB Portland-Weymouth, winning warm acknowledgements from the United States…"For over a year your island of Portland has been a key factor in the movement of troops and their weapons to the far shore in the liberation of the Continent…"

Portland's Royal Naval base was closed down in the 1990s at the end of the Cold War. What was the huge RNAS helicopter base is now Osprey Quay and the Weymouth and Portland National Sailing Academy. Yachts line the harbour where warships once anchored. Today, Portland and Weymouth earn their living from the leisure industry and provided an excellent venue for the maritime events in the 2012 Olympic Games.

Above: The statue of King George III on the seafront at Weymouth.

Dorset and the Seaside Holiday

Dorset pioneered seaside holidays. Ralph Allen, famous for developing Bath as a fashionable spa, brought his ailing wife to Weymouth to try the then novel sea bathing cure in 1750 – complemented by sea water drinking. However, it was King George III who gave Weymouth the royal patronage that made it nationally known and at a time when Continental travel was impossible because of war.

Visiting Weymouth in 1789, the King found his health much improved. Between then and 1805, the Royal Family made fourteen visits to the resort, enjoying bathing, yachting and inland excursions. George discarded pomp and dressed informally, rubbing shoulders with the townsfolk, who peered in through the windows of Gloucester Lodge, his seafront home, to see what he ate for breakfast. True, there were some concessions to idle ceremony, though the king's heart was never in it. His bathing machine (a replica is on Weymouth seafront) was decorated with the British flag and the Royal Coat of Arms. When His Majesty emerged from the briny after his first historic dip he was ambushed by a patriotic band playing "God save great George our King".

Sailing gave George an excuse to avoid further such embarrassments. At that time, sailing for pleasure was as novel as sea bathing, but Dorset with its fine harbours and splendid coastline was well suited to fostering both. Bournemouth, which developed rapidly under the patronage of Captain Lewis Tregonwell, enjoyed its first regatta in 1844. Sail races at Weymouth and Christchurch followed. The Royal Dorset Yacht Club was founded in 1875, the first of a series of clubs catering for a growing sport.

Paddle steamers arrived in Weymouth in 1857. Swanage, Bournemouth, Poole, Lulworth, Weymouth and Lyme offered cruises along

Below: The ammonite pavement on Monmouth Beach, Lyme Regis. The fossils here draw thousands of tourists every year as well as professional collectors.

Above: Weymouth Beach, with some of the best sand anywhere in Britain!

the coast. Crossings to the Channel Islands and France followed. Boat trips remain popular, along with other classic British holiday staples such as seaside promenades; the Victorian piers at Bournemouth and Swanage and Punch and Judy shows on Weymouth sands.

Newer seaside attractions including sailboarding and windsurfing are popular too, whilst the Jurassic Coast and Lyme Regis in particular are famous for geology and fossils. Our understanding of "deep time"; the earth's age, origins and development, owe much to the pioneering work of Lyme fossil collector Mary Anning (1799-1847). Despite her modest education and humble background Mary's discoveries, including the first ichthyosaur to be correctly identified and the first two plesiosaur skeletons ever found, gained the attention and respect of leading Victorian geologists.

Meanwhile, great social and industrial changes were under way, bringing the story of the Dorset coast into the modern age. At first, only the leisured elite could imitate George III in affording the luxury of seaside vacations, but they were joined by growing numbers of middle and later working class visitors as Victorian Britain's burgeoning industrial wealth trickled down the social scale and paid holidays became general.

Railways made Dorset resorts affordable and accessible as never before. Weymouth joined the rapidly growing national network in 1857, shortly followed by Poole, Bournemouth and Christchurch; Swanage in 1885 and Lyme Regis in 1903.

Forward to the Present and into the Future

Tourism and the associated leisure industry grew through the twentieth century to take centre stage in the evolving story of the Dorset coast, yet the other actors continue to play their parts.

Dorset still plays a significant role in national defence, although its military use has inevitably declined since the Second World War and with Britain's altered world position. Since the closure of Portland's naval facilities, it is focussed on the Army's training grounds at Bovington and the coastal ranges around Lulworth.

Smuggling, dominant during the eighteenth and early nineteenth centuries continues also, albeit on a smaller scale and with its focus changed from overtaxed luxuries to more lucrative narcotics - as irregular reports of Revenue hauls show. Legal trade too remains important; fishing boats and merchant craft mix with the yachts and pleasure boats that outnumber them in Dorset's ports and harbours, which have all adapted to time and changing circumstances.

Below left: Gad Cliff west of Kimmeridge. This spectacular coastline is still in the care of the army and part of the important Lulworth Ranges. Smugglers used to haul kegs of brandy up these cliffs.

Below right: The pretty harbour at West Bay, home to fishing boats and leisure craft. Also well known as the setting for the television drama Broadchurch.

Main picture: The paddle steamer Waverley in Swanage Bay.

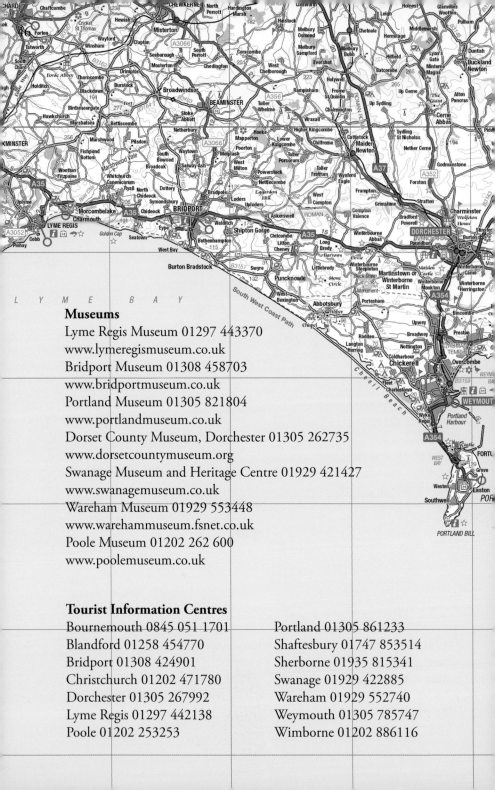

Museums

Lyme Regis Museum 01297 443370
www.lymeregismuseum.co.uk
Bridport Museum 01308 458703
www.bridportmuseum.co.uk
Portland Museum 01305 821804
www.portlandmuseum.co.uk
Dorset County Museum, Dorchester 01305 262735
www.dorsetcountymuseum.org
Swanage Museum and Heritage Centre 01929 421427
www.swanagemuseum.co.uk
Wareham Museum 01929 553448
www.warehammuseum.fsnet.co.uk
Poole Museum 01202 262 600
www.poolemuseum.co.uk

Tourist Information Centres

Bournemouth 0845 051 1701
Blandford 01258 454770
Bridport 01308 424901
Christchurch 01202 471780
Dorchester 01305 267992
Lyme Regis 01297 442138
Poole 01202 253253

Portland 01305 861233
Shaftesbury 01747 853514
Sherborne 01935 815341
Swanage 01929 422885
Wareham 01929 552740
Weymouth 01305 785747
Wimborne 01202 886116

Army Ranges

The coast between Lulworth and Kimmeridge is part of the army ranges. It is only open at certain times; most weekends and during the school holidays. Check on www.dorsetforyou.com/lulworth-range-walks or phone 01929 404819.

Select Bibliography

Ashley, Harry, *The Dorset Coast, History, Lore and Legend,* Countryside Books, Newbury, 1992.

Hesketh, Robert, *Legends and Folklore of Dorset,* Inspiring Places Publishing, Alderholt, 2013.

Hesketh, Robert, *Devon Smugglers, The Truth Behind the Fiction,* Bossiney Books, Launceston, 2007 and 2010.

Le Pard, Gordon, *Dorset and the Sea,* Dorset Books, Wellington, 2010.

Morley, Geoffrey, *Smuggling in Hampshire and Dorset 1700-1850,* Countryside Books, Newbury, 1983.

Street, Sean, *Tales of Old Dorset,* Countryside Books, Newbury, 1985.

Westwood, Robert, *Smugglers' Dorset,* Inspiring Places Publishing, Alderholt, 2007.

Books by Inspiring Places

Ancient Dorset
Legends and Folklore of Dorset
Fossils and Rocks of the Jurassic Coast
The Tyneham Story
A Guide to the Beaches and Coves of Dorset
Jurassic Coast Fossils
Dark Age Dorset
A brief guide to Purbeck
Purbeck Walks
Walking West Dorset
A brief guide to Sherborne, Shaftesbury and Blandford
A brief guide to Weymouth, Portland and Dorchester
The Life and Works of Thomas Hardy
Mystery Big Cats of Dorset
Day Tours in the East of Dorset
The Jurassic Coast Illustrated

All photographs by the author except pg. 10,11 - Verity Hesketh, pgs. 2,33,42 and 44 (inset) by Robert Westwood.
Front cover: Mupe Rocks (Robert Westwood)
Rear cover: Weymouth Harbour (author)